AF245593

Mark Roper

24. 4. 05

BY THE SAME AUTHOR

The Hen Ark
(Peterloo/Salmon, 1990)

Catching the Light
(Peterloo, 1996)

The Home Fire
(Abbey Press, 1998)

WHEREABOUTS

—

Mark Roper

Abbey Press ◆ Peterloo

First published in April 2005 in an edition of 1,000 copies
250 of which are signed and numbered by the author

Abbey Press
Newry Office
Courtenay Hill
Newry, County Down
Northern Ireland
BT34 2ED
www.abbeypressbooks.com

◆

Peterloo Poets
The Old Chapel
Sand Lane
Calstock, Cornwall
PL18 9QX
United Kingdom
www.peterloopoets.com

A CIP record for this book is available from the British Library

ISBN: 1 901617 24 6 (Abbey Press)
ISBN: 1 904324 30 4 (Peterloo Poets)
Author: Roper, Mark
Title: Whereabouts
Format: 138 mm x 214 mm
2005

Design: Adrian Rice
Cover Image: *The Crow Field*, (detail), 2004 by Jean Clyne, 60 x 60 cms, oil on linen
Typesetting by David Anderson in 11/13pt Sabon
Printed by Nicholson & Bass Ltd, Belfast

CONTENTS

for

Ted and Mary O'Regan

HIM

So many people claim to know him well.
They tell you stories which make perfect sense.
These are his habits. His hobbies. His friends.
Address? Photo? Belongings? Look. Right here.

Of course it wasn't always plain sailing.
It appears that X led to Y. That if
he'd only done A instead of B,
C couldn't possibly have happened.

There was something unique about him.
It was his way of talking. His silence.
The way he did whatever he did. Etcetera.
You'd know when you'd been in his company.

When this stranger claims, as he will, to be
your self, on no account believe him.
Dates, names, events, will coincide. The rest
is made up. You know it wasn't like that.

Send him on his way with a good thrashing.
Let the moon and stars weigh down your tongue.
Envy their solitudes. Do not pretend
you are anything other than lonely.

WOODPECKER

You come home and tell me you've seen,
for the first time, a woodpecker,
feeding at the coconut shell
hung in your brother-in-law's tree.

What kind was it I want to know.
There are 3 kinds, black, green, spotted.
One laughs, it's known as a yaffle.
There aren't any in Ireland.

You can't remember its colour.
It flew slowly down to the tree,
edged its way out towards the shell,
began to eat, you can see it now

and you shape it in the air for me,
one hand carefully cupping
the weight of what it meant,
you hold it there for me as if

I'd never broken anything
you'd ever given me and it starts
to cross the space between us
and I do not know what to say.

SWALLOW

A spent firework
on the lawn.

Tiny feet still
nailed to space.

Wings wind-sleek.
Head sleek with wind.

So full of flight
it must have died

of ripeness.
In the tail's V

a stalk of sky.

SPEAKING OF HORSES

Morning finds them asleep, wrapped in each other,
breath clouding over long skulls. Eyes open
to flood their frames with world in their way known.

Untangled, an improbable balancing act complete,
they pour themselves into grass. Then, as if
at a signal, they start to canter: first one,

then the rest, always in a curve across the field,
streamlined by the air they part. Abruptly
pulled up, an arrested blaze, they settle –

great pieces of furniture which could never canter.
And then they canter again, hooves barely seeming
to touch the ground, a fluent surge of purpose

halted sharply in an afterspray of broken chestnut.
It lingers on the air like a trace of thought.
And then they canter again. And then they pull up,

and there's no stopping it, no stopping it at all,
what happens turning into what is said to happen,
what is said to happen becoming what happens.

And then they canter again. And then they pull up.
And the field is filled with something that reaches
but melts on the tongue. And then they canter again.

SKIP

At the end of a long night you drive home
to the house you know is empty, but warm.
You'll let yourself relax, doze by the fire.
Just one stop to make on the way home,
to chuck the rubbish into a factory skip.
You drive quietly into the car park:
the lights are still on in the factory,
you know you're not supposed to use their skip.
Unlock the boot, heave the bag up and away.
Get back in to start the car – find you've no keys.
Realize you've chucked them away with the bag,
into twelve deep feet of tangled rubbish.
You can't ask the factory men for help.
There's no one at home and you're miles from it.
You sit in the car. Misled by a streetlamp
into thinking it's day, a bird starts to sing.
You open the window to hear it better.
It's the robin, you seem to remember,
gets fooled like that. Or is it the chaffinch?

THE TOY MUSEUM

Glassed in at the turn of the stairs
leading up to the Toy Museum,
all shapes and sizes, some patched,
others good as new, they're all seated,
all staring straight ahead.

And all have their arms outstretched,
as if their children had just left,
as if at any moment those children,
the Bonzoes and the Bunties,
the Jimjams, the Jenjens, might return,

as if time and flesh could be rewound
and they could all come streaming back,
out of the earth and out of the fire,
through white hair, wounds, weddings,
into suits of innocence, this embrace.

And no one can tell the bears how
the years add themselves to the years,
how children go raining into the dark.
Love blazing off their golden coats,
absence burning in their arms, they stare on.

FOOTFALL

by the lake
alder birch
green deeps

two bottles
butts a lighter
in the dirt

cool shadow
insect and
bird song

lightfall
meadowsweet
a grebe dives

broken shell
in the mud
one feather

thin air
flame set
under leaf

heron cross
cross the lake
again

water teach
cover me grass
and continue

HOME

Goodbye you had to say to every room
when as a child you went out – those rooms
might not be there when you returned.

Even now, when you've been out, you like
to creep back and stare through your windows –
as if to catch the rooms by surprise.

To see what they look like in your absence.
Or to snatch a glimpse of yourself – the house
a mirror which might make that self seem true.

It's you, you, the one that lives here, you want
it to say; the more you look the harder
you are to find. You see books on their shelves,

spoons in drawers, everything in its right place –
but you know they're not talking about you.
They forget you as soon as you leave.

You stare into your reflection, trapped
inside the glass, neither here nor there.
A stranger always you were, you will be.

SUIT

A butterfly
on a windowsill –
a child's suit.

The suit which fitted
so perfectly
when I was young.

The one I thought
would grow with me.

The only one
ever that
fitted properly.

My life,
where did it go?

My life
that did not grow.

VERDICT

Sometimes you look at someone
who is looking another way and
suddenly they turn and stare straight
through you – as if they knew not
only that you'd been looking
but knew more about you
than you'll ever know yourself.
You feel pinned down but tell yourself
it was only a look, after all.

◆

Sometimes someone will say something
to you, or about you, and part
of you will hear so deeply you will
never be the same again.
You become what they have said.
Someone says something to you
in a room and part of you sits there
in that room for the rest of your life,
and never questions that this should be so.

◆

And should someone find their way
down to the door of that room,
(a room you don't know is there,
it's buried so deep), and knock
and knock until they gain entry,
can what's been hurt stir?
Can it rise from its chair and let
itself be led up all those stairs,
can it stand again in frightening light,
bear the loving hand on its skin?

AND THIS IS TRUE

And this is true too, a young fox ambling
through pink campion, bluebell, ramson
on a spring evening.

Despite everything, what's been, what will come,
the violence, the murder, the terrible news,
a vivid burn of fur,

a beautiful face, are also true. Dare you say
it seems not to have a care in the world?
It seems not to.

You're making this up of course: the fox
walks in a trace of your making, your eyes
impose this pattern.

And it's no more true than the heavy fox
you dragged off the road by its tail,
its face a smashed fruit.

No more true than the fox breaking into
the henhouse, tearing all the heads
off all the chickens.

Than what your country did to others.
Than the buried children. Than hunger. Than all
you have to answer for,

than all those with neither time nor freedom
to stop to watch a fox in thick flower
amble towards them.

And there are so many. And it's true
the fox will see you, turn and run,
eyes full of fear.

Now it ambles towards you, through campion,
bluebell, ramson, on a spring evening.
Do not doubt it.

SLEEPING WITH THE KINGFISHER

Its appearance in the bed wasn't surprising.
Giraldus said a dead one kept linen fresh.

No, what surprised was the size of the thing
and the way it hugged me close to its breast.

To feel its bill run the rule down my spine.
To be enfolded in sapphire wings. Surprising.

How much more so to wake and find myself ablaze,
my heart the blue seed in a blossom of flame.

THE INNER POET

Hi, it's me. Yes, I know
this is an awkward time.
And it's getting longer
the more you listen to me.

I know you're up there
in front of an audience
hoping to look calm,
trying to look inspired.

That's why I'm here in fact.
I'd like to help. Let's start
with an old reminder.
One from the childhood.

Carol concert wasn't it?
You were picked to sing solo.
Only picked because
your Dad was the vicar.

You started the show.
But your voice wouldn't
do what you wanted it to.
You sounded like a fool.

Remember how everyone
stared at you? Course you do.
How you cried? Bad,
wasn't it, bad as could be.

You often say you'll never
get over that moment.
You're probably right.
Gottago. Have a good one.

THE HOSPITAL FOYER

Sooner or later everyone I know
will come through here. Already, it seems,
in the café, at the shop, in the toilets,
all the faces I meet are known to me.

I greet a friend and tell her how well
she's looking. We both know I'm lying.
From his eyes I try to gauge whether
to ask another what he's doing here.

He has time yet not to have to answer.
His life is still in his own hands.
This is a place to linger, to put the moment off
before you join the long continuous streams

to the wards, the clinics: before the crowd
singles out into their separate journeys
and you're alone in a quieter corridor
which seems to concentrate on you,

seems to know already what's the matter
as you head to a bedside, a bed,
an appointment, a diagnosis, an all-clear,
an unclear, a not-good, a darkness.

Sooner or later I will see myself,
through the army of last-ditch smokers,
approach the glass doors. I will see
my own reflection come to meet me.

I will be afraid but there will be
someone I know, I will be made welcome:
entrance here is so easy to gain,
all you need your own, or another's, pain.

THE FIRST MOVE

When the grids you slot them into dissolve,
think how people always surprise you.
Always better, kinder, than you allowed.
Think how each suffers as much and more than you.

Think how you love the things of this world.
The birds, the stone, the flowers, the water.
Everything that cannot love you back.
How easy to love the wordless wild and dead.

Your father said he believed in mercy,
not forgiveness. You never forgave him.
Think how the heart hardens in its cage,
repeating its moves. You must learn how to love.

DIGESTION

Since it all comes down to digestion,
one thing's growth another thing's decay,
it's just as well those bitter juices
do their job unseen, just as well
that animals crawl into the dark to die,
just as well the ground makes such short work.
Thank the thoughtful eye for the way
it looks to heal this breaking world
and since one thing so quickly becomes
another, learn to cherish examples
of the most gentle digestion:
the suede shoe stood on its own so long
in a field, sole being parted
with such infinite care from upper;
or, in that monastery crypt, the way
the tomb of a monk buried in a wall
has been opened, and a spotlight picks out
his old bones: a dark crumble of honey.

RED ADMIRALS

Of the reddened leaves
drifting to earth
three or four seem
jerked into life,

soft, erratic flames
wandering on wings
too gorgeous for gravity.

Drunk on windfall
they settle
on a white wall,

bloody fingerprints,
small fires
on the edge of night.

The world wheels
under pitiless stars
into dark –

after such dark
what colour
can there be?

A robin's dull ember
in the wreck
of a tree.

ENTRIES

Falcons, we thought. Blunt tails and curved wings
fooled us as the birds swung across a distant cliff.

Swifts we knew them for close-up: alpine swifts,
riding on the updraughts off the limestone,

breasts half-mooned as if rubbed clean
by the light and heat beating off water and stone.

We watched them until they flew inside us.
Though we'll forget them they'll never leave,

flying at the mention of their name,
coming at odd intervals unbidden.

Not just as remembered but part now too
of what remembers them. Entered

by the light of our watching them together.

THE HOME FIRE

Saturday dusks, Eddie Waring warbling on
before the wrestling, then the football results,
magical names, Hotspur to Hamilton Academicals.

The smell of new mud from boots drying by the fire,
its tile surround adorned by biblical scenes,
the jawbone of an ass, that hairy man Esau,

and the fire heaped with tarblocks that crackled
and spat so much they turned us all into goalies,
diving around to extinguish smouldering carpet.

Fighting later for a place on the leather sofa
whose brass studs could make you see stars,
and one night allowed to stay up late to watch

Johanssen fight Patterson, live, our reflections
and the fireglow dancing in the small screen,
all of us there, in and out of the glass.

Then the long trek to bed, across the cold flags
of the hall, ice of air shaken by a huge clock's
erratic tick, shadows thick with menace.

Up the stairs, never touching the two iron rungs
in the wooden bannister, running past the ghost
at the turn of the steps, across the landing

and safe into bed. Just to lie there then,
cradled by the rhythms of the Northern trains,
watching headlights polish the ceiling. Waking

to hear doves crooning, sunlight at the curtains
with a sack of golden air; waking to find
the room gone, adults gone, fire out, roof off,

darkness and stars raining down on my bared head.

SATURDAY MORNING

Saturday morning, tea in the pot,
cats on a quilt worn past repair.

Outside the window, the low hills,
stony light, horses in Kearns's field.

Old dried leaf, fresh water. Given cups.
Dust motes in steam. Touch of known skin.

Skin that we're shy of all over again.
That we try to hide from each other.

Which sags, has wrinkles, is mottled.
From which things need to be cut out.

Bodies once so well known to us,
now unknown. Which let us down.

Bodies we're ashamed of, angry about,
find difficult to accept as ours.

Which are no longer possessed
but possess us, at times disgust.

Not the bodies we fell in love with,
couldn't wait to undress.

This was happening all the time,
behind the screens of desire, seen clearly now.

Bodies which have hurt each other,
grown old and tired with compromise.

Which have stuck with each other
and would not recover if separated now.

Which must not be left alone, needing
more than ever now to be loved.

Tea in the pot. Old dried leaf, fresh water.
Given cups. Us two, in deep.

PLAIN SAILING

They were just where you said they'd be, the owls,
ghosting the lowness, all grab and glamour,
flaring off the dykes like match flames.

There as if you'd turned a switch, to light up
a small room whose exact contents you knew.
Enough so to glimpse them working the flat fields,

to drive back to the house and let their image
develop; the May silvers, the whitethroats
we'd seen focused in that savage sweetness.

Next day the balloon came over, seemed to drop
slowly down towards the house, until an arm
appeared, tiny, pointing towards the house.

A jet of fire: puffed up, the balloon rose
and travelled on, so calm we might have thought
there could be such a thing as plain sailing –

the grass turning into fields, the fields
into farms – these things growing clearer,
brighter, the more they begin to fade.

FOR ALL YOU KNOW

For all you know
you might need the eye
of the little egret

bent on these fields,
a refuge from storm,
for the first time.

Assume its reception
above the hedged lanes,
the drowning river.

Let its yellow toe
root in corners,
queer the pitch.

Bring its black beak
to bear on the pane
of the flood-puddle:

to muddy the water,
to cloud the issue
for all you know.

STARLING

Starlings join to make one single-minded machine.
Whatever tree they land on
becomes a starling tree.

Above the railway line great flocks flow from shape to shape,
black lakes which flatten, tilt,
stretch, turn over, fold.

It would appear they cannot bear to be parted.
Tonight one gone astray
divebombs the bird table.

A nosey, nasty crowd of one, soon it's driven
all the other birds away.
No more come. Then what?

It shoots across the garden, jabs its unchoired beak
into the bird box.
No one there. So now?

Twitches. Looks around. Looks out across the fields.
All the unconverted air.
The horrid unblack blue.

Takes off its coat. Why not? Unfastens beak and bone.
Loses sight of itself.
Starts a new life. Alone.

LEAF

Pontevedra, August '96, it reads,
this dried leaf picked up in a park,
inscribed, kept for a bookmark.

Taken for granted now, colour faded,
fabric starting to tatter, leafliness
so lost in function it comes as

a shock to see, accidentally held
against bright sun, how the leaf
turns into an x-ray of itself.

Such intricate veining and staining.
Such detailed, unknowable history.
Such private life, such suchness

in this leaf, held in this hand,
in this field of sunlight and shadow.
At this moment. In this life.

Leaf of the hand, leaf of touch.
Leaf of light, of air, leaf of sight.
Leaf of emptiness. Leaf of form.

Leaf of the burning terrible holy world.

FACE

When boiling soup splashed up
to scald your cheek, that was
one shock. When people moved
to avoid your bandaged glare
in a bar, that was another.
Face changed, you were changed.

As a child I wondered which face
I would wear in heaven: my then face,
my adult one, my old age one?
And what about parents, friends?
Which ones would they be wearing?
How would anyone be recognized?

Faces won't matter, I was told.
Spirits don't have them.
Even then I suspected no one
could exist without flesh:
face, spirit, were not separate
nor would either be saved.

On the tiny field of new skin
around your eye, a soft gold down
grows again. When you're cold
or tired, the slight scar darkens:
as if death had held you, admired,
left a fingerprint, a maker's mark.

RAIN

This freckle
of rain on the roof,
it's the gentlest siege,
not wanting
to come in, nor disturb
our sleep, seeming
to lose interest, fading
then coming back,
a quiet insistence,
someone touching
unexpectedly
your arm as they speak,
the faintest of faint
invitations
to follow, to spread
out over broken
oak leaves,
over purple stones
and sleeping birds,
to lose face,
be dispersed.

CUCKOO

When I crossed to the island I found
the cuckoo had followed me over.
It sang at the edge of the wood,
it sang through the root of the clover.

Was it saying all flesh is grass?
Was it crying for love of its ground?
Did it only repeat what it heard?
Was there sorrow or mock in that sound?

If it called and it called for a mate,
why still calling long after she'd gone?
That call which wrings the old flesh,
long after its will can be done.

NEED

All day I've tidied you away:
the bath's ghost of scented steam,
a tap's dye ring, your weight from cushions,
your shape from the bed.

All day I've worn your presence away
as if hunting some seamless silence
out of which you can't be shaken,
some place where you might survive
with no outward or visible sign.

At night, when silence won't answer back,
in the mirror I see the boy trained
not to cry, taught mercy not forgiveness,
who must not show his hurt,
who must prove he can do without you.

All day I've tidied his need away.

CAREER

The boy lies full-length
on a green-painted pew
in a corner of the garden,

one hand on a stick
nailed into its wood,
the control for this rocket

from whose window shrinks
the voices and faces
of those who love him,

the anxious concern,
the expectation,
the chart of his course.

Now he can take it all in:
the circuits of amber
that night makes of cities,

the poster-paint fields,
the soft nose of land
dipped in a saucer of sea;

now he is weightless,
a space in which these things
can see themselves.

He lets go of the stick,
disconnects his mike.
The calls for re-entry

will not get through.
From such a career
how should he return,

to be known again,
to be the boy
his family think he is;

how forget all this space;
how fit himself
back into his face?

THE BROKEN FIELDS

Driving home through the dark
an owl slides past the windscreen.

Fearing I might have hit it
I stop, get out to look –
only an old paper bag.

Only a grieving wind.
Only fields stretching away,
the broken fields, aching
in their chemical chains.

VAN GOGH'S *THE FARM*

Where does it come from, this farm
and the light which wraps this farm
in sage blessing, light of welcome return?

When it was never my life to cross a field
at dusk, to open a blue door, to know
the squeak of its latch and the way

it's being listened for with love,
why should it all seem so familiar?
Why second nature to take water from a water-sweated jug,

to know each stair's creak, to feel worn sheets
roughly cool my skin, to watch shadows
house and unhouse the sloped ceiling?

Look at those figures crossing the yard,
how their lives seem to have shaped them
to their own shapes, shapes intended:

they travel in air that fits them, through light
that loves them, in joined and finished life.
They will always know where they are going.

PECK

After six years of living as a pair
one hen sickened, hunched up, as if
trying to climb back inside herself.
The other bird stood over her, on guard,
fussing, attentive, concerned, it seemed.
Close-up I could see she was pecking,
pulling out feathers around the neck
of the sick bird, baring flesh to eat.

I shouldn't have been surprised.
Everything lives off something else.
Flesh, bones, rocks, soil, selves, days,
what can they be made of but lives?
What's the great sun in all its glory
but a lustrous hen, pecking us, itself, away?

THE ROBIN

For days it kept on tapping at the window,
a spent coal trying to regain a fire,
a little glowing boat beating against
a wall of surf, a frozen sheet of spray.

When we opened the window, in it flew.
Began, it seemed, to search, as if for what
had been there when it was out, but now
was out when it was in. Soon it was tapping

at the window again, from the inside, as if
the real thing was to cross that barrier,
as if the real world lay beyond
and it were living in a realm of shadow.

When you read it was after its reflection,
thinking it a rival, or a partner,
we saw that image growing in its head,
an ideal bird in an ideal space, we saw

the little robin storm the gates of heaven
and find itself bewildered and alone,
finding that heavens depend upon not
being entered, there being no other side.

We might have seen it homeless then, flying
back into a world suddenly strange,
provisional, a stage set to be ransacked
for hints of another, better place –

but it flew straight into its world, its home,
straight into its struggle and its song.
In the window, looking on, we saw ourselves:
in our minds that glass, that image entered.

JOHN CONDON

Stamped into still supple leather, clear as day,
the number you were assigned: 6322.
It's said you joined up for a pair of boots.
By those boots alone you were recognized.

It's said, to enlist at Clonmel, you fled
the stink and crush of Wheelbarrow Lane.
Wangled your way into a draft for France.
Killed May 1915, Bellevarde Ridge.

Lasted one week. Little statistic,
lost in the ledgers of slaughter on slaughter,
it's said, at fourteen, you were the youngest
of the millions to die in that war.

How high it would rise above you, how
it hides you, the ridge of that war's dead.
Number's all we can trick you out in:
1 week. 14 years. Ist World War. Millions.

One star burning in the dark of a well.
Fourteen white flowers on an apple branch.
The first swallow's skimming return.
In a poppy capsule, a million seeds.

SWAN HOUSE

1

And what were we to make of that swan
which came crashing through the mist, low
over the house like a lost glory,
so sudden it was gone before it came,
re-assumed into mist, its light
only seeming to reach us then, as if
we only saw it when we breathed the word *Swan*,
as if all recognition were farewell.

2

Slower than sound but faster than words
it came, an echo preceding its source,
the mist rhythmed, strained to breaking
until sound was above us, the air
hallowed by a steady magnificent applause
which drew us up and in until
we both were and were received into
the house of our astonished praise.

STOCK

Inside the winter-bare apple tree,
I thought as I was cutting it down,
blossom and fruit must somehow exist,
all the way back to the very first apple.

I was breaking in to that succession.
So when the saw hopped, and blood sapped my thumb,
I knew this was more than the tree's attempt
to stop my cutting – more than mere revenge.

I considered myself grafted on to. Attached
to my thumb the possibility of blossom.

MAGWITCH

If I went out in a peasouper fog
I'd have to wear a hankie over my mouth.

Later, where my mouth had been, I'd find
a dark stain, in the shape of a kiss.

Out there, lost at first, I'd learnt
to find my way from one lamppost to the next.

It all seemed crazy in daylight. Crazy
how one night Magwitch followed me

out of the T.V. into the fog, crazy
how his hand reached to clutch my ankle.

If I lifted my hankie, if I didn't cry out,
was it because I knew, even then,

I'd sooner breathe poison
than risk betrayal of that hand?

Father on whose love I choke, love me.

SNIPE

That small heart
plunged through our own.

All over the sky
these scars of sound,
this listening.

Where we could
never be,
but were.

ALL OF ME

So all of me, why not take all of me –
the one with so many certificates,
the failure, the one who can't cope,
the boy who never grew up,
the boy who grew up too early;

strong silent one, son-but-not-father,
one who believes, one who'd like to,
one who can't, one who'd never say,
he who never shows his feelings,
he who wears his heart on his sleeve;

man who cannot cry, inner child,
buffoon, kind man, the good boy,
only-as-good-as-his-next-joke boy,
the guy who at certain moments,
that other fellow, and all the rest;

him who lets it all flow over him,
him crippled by disappointment,
the liar, the cheat, stranger on the C.V.,
Mr. Polite, Mr. Charm, Mr. Bitter, Mr. Vague,
and all the others you'll say I've left out;

the one who likes you one who doesn't,
one who'll touch you the one who won't,
one who'll get carried away, one who'll watch,
the judge, the jury, the one on trial,
the innocent victim, the guilty as charged,

o all of me why not take all of me

ELDER

I come home these nights under such light,
alleys of softly glowing elder
in whose flower the bridal whites discolour,
spring-freshness sours into summer.

Rubbledrudge, thicketskivvy, your mild moons
wax where they're left, part of the undergrowth,
swagged with bramble, woodbine, taken for granted
and only too content to leave it that way.

Elder, if you deign to enter this poem
who could blame you? Our ancient hatred haunts,
hovers like a cloud of summer flies.
God's stinking tree, you had much to answer for.

On your wood Christ was crucified, Judas hanged.
Boats made of elder sunk, cradles sickened.
The hand of a man struck with elder sprouted
from its grave. What did you do wrong?

Hazy status earned you hate. Neither bush
nor tree, never straight nor strong. Stems thick
but hollow. Scent half-piss, half-champagne.
Such uncertainty could only mean one thing.

How have you answered our thought's poison?
Found the common ground. Bent your elbows.
Fed the winter thrush with your berries.
Spun these discs of chalky clotted light.

Asked nothing. Asked only to be what you are.
Not like anything. Not like anything at all.

HARRIERS

You might see a marsh harrier, the warden said.
But that's all. Wrong season. Worst time of day.

We walked to the tower, through fierce noon heat.
Climbed up. Stood. Stared. At nothing. All we saw
was that marsh harrier, once, in the distance.

'If we hurry,' you said, 'we might just catch
the ten-to-four bus.' 'We'll never make it,'
I said, 'it's gone 2.' 'So what do you suggest?'
'There's a way back through the reeds,
look here on the map.' 'That'll take hours –
we've no food, no water.' 'Have it your way.'
'No, we'll try the reeds.' 'No, I don't want to.'

Half-running back, through still fierce heat,
hating our selves as much as each other,
checking watches again and again, we just
made it, fell straight into hysterical sleep,
jerking awake, sweat spitting out of our heads.

Behind us lay the reedbeds. The huge sky.
The green canal. Yellow waterlilies.
Emptiness. The ten thousand things.

HERON

Every now and then, often at dusk
as if to darken the darkness of dark,

over the house a heron wrings out
its terrible cry: a note, long pondered,

exactly the same as all preceding, all
to come, to add to that lifelong solo

whose scale, slowness, lack of closure,
whose unchanging survey and sum of sorrow

and sadness and sadness and sorrow,
whose utter lack of meaning and hope

make even the most heart-rending lament
seem child's play, merest self-pity.

WHEREABOUTS

Take the road under
the twisting oaks
when the mountain turns
so blue you think
you can see through it.

◆

Beside the bridge
winter heliotrope,
a visitor from India,
sets out its stall.
Mimulus from China
spills its seed
on the stream.

◆

Two stone piers
astray in a field –
on which side
was the way in?

◆

A blackbird's slither
and scald,
a wren's rattle.

◆

The beat of my heart
going, in the silence,
its own way.

◆

Crooked gorse –
on its sleeve
one too many
hearts of gold.

◆

A burnt log,
a Snowcream carton,
evergreen branches,
flattened verge rising:
no camp continues.

◆

Whose are they,
eyes, hands, voice,
the thoughts that build,
the thoughts that build?

◆

On a breeze
the ghost of snipe,
of woodcock
enough and to spare.

◆

Drained obedient fields,
water's tame trickle
through concrete pipes.
Overhead a satellite
counts the cows.

◆

Miraculous wound,
the roses that still flower
where a house once was.

◆

In the horse's eye,
nothing rests.

◆

Ballyglassoon, Dowlin,
Tobernafauna, Cahill's Hill.

◆

Over the tall grass
swallows dip and dive,
one minute here,
the next gone.

◆

Limestone, lichen,
dandelion, cloud, all
in their own good time.

◆

New bungalows rising
out of the ground
overnight, ivy
stripped off
the old demesne wall.

◆

A heron's cry,
sileage bales
like gorged torsos.

◆

The fields that run
through my head
are still the fields,
sodden after rain.

◆

Cow parsley holds
a ruined head to sun –
a saint, nicotine brown,
smoked to the butt by God.

◆

Whose life turns out
the way they meant it to?
Who knows whose turn
it is to die?

◆

Fruit at its feet
the crab tree implores,
beggar who knows it wiser
to give than receive.

◆

Look back the way
you came: the more
you look the less
it leads to you.

◆

By the No Dumping sign
a fridge, some shoes,
two armchairs.
In the dyke
a dead pig.

◆

A squashed crow's wing
lifts and waves
in the wake of a passing car.

◆

How deeply
everything forgets
I was ever here.

◆

Butterfly orchids,
fifteen this year
in Tom Quinn's field.

◆

Love for these things
becomes the prayer
you offer to all
that is not thing.

◆

A ram's horn
on the grass,
a comma linking
future to past.

◆

A wind you can't see
roughs to silver
first one patch of grass,
then another.

Acknowledgements

Acknowledgements are due to the editors of the following publications in which some of these poems, or versions of them, have appeared: *Chapman, College Green, Decies, Film and Film Culture, Ink Bottle, Metre, Planet, Poetry Ireland, The Backyards of Heaven, the living stream, The Rialto, THE SHOp, The Stony Thursday Book, Tabla, Wildeside, A Wing and a Prayer.*

Nine of these poems appeared in *The Home Fire*, Abbey Press, 1998.

The author records grateful thanks to Le Château de Lavigny and the Tyrone Guthrie Centre, Annaghmakerrig.

Abbey Press gratefully acknowledge the support of their Patrons: Seamus Heaney, Padraig and Nicky McGuinness, Gerard Trainor and Martin Quinn.